Colette and the Watch of Time: Newark

By Dave Fargher

A long time ago, in the very heart of England, nestled beside the wide, winding waters of the River Trent, lay a little town called Newark-on-Trent. But this wasn't just any town; it was a place steeped in history, a vibrant tapestry woven with tales of mighty castles, powerful kings, fierce battles, and the everyday lives of countless people stretching back through time.

Newark's story began not with grand declarations, but with humble beginnings. It started as a simple resting point for weary travelers on the ancient Roman road, the Fosse Way. Over centuries, it blossomed, especially after a powerful bishop decided to build a magnificent castle there in the 1100s.

This towering fortress, strategically placed by the river, became the town's guardian, its silent sentinel watching over Newark and its people.

Even today, though time has worn its walls, the impressive ruins of Newark Castle stand as a testament to its past, inviting you to step inside and imagine the clatter of knights' armour and the decrees of kings echoing through its stone corridors.

Centuries later, in the tumultuous 1600s, Newark found itself thrust onto the national stage during the brutal conflict known as the English Civil War. It became a fiercely loyal stronghold, defending the King's cause with unwavering bravery.

The town endured three devastating sieges, each a testament to the courage and resilience of its inhabitants who refused to surrender easily.

Walk through Newark today, and you can still find whispers of those battles, subtle reminders of a time when cannon fire echoed through its streets.

Today, Newark-on-Trent is a vibrant, peaceful market town. Its bustling markets, fascinating museums, and the breathtaking architecture of St Mary Magdalene Church offer a wonderful blend of old and new. It's a perfect place to immerse yourself in history, explore ancient buildings that have stood for centuries, and simply enjoy a leisurely walk along the tranquil riverbanks.

This is one girl's magical story... a journey through time itself.

Chapters

1. Introduction - Colette's Discovery

2. The Ice Age: Mammoth Mishaps and Flinty Fun (14,000 years ago)

2.

3. The Timber Circle: Ancient Raves and Sacred Spaces (4,000 years ago)

4. Roman Margidunum: Toasty Toes and Twelve Goats (43-410 AD)

5. Early St. Mary Magdalene Church: Mud, Mortar, and Monks (c. 11th Century)

6. Newark Castle's Construction: Bishops, Battlements, and Builders (12th Century)

7. King John at Newark Castle: Whispers of Loss and Royal Ill-Fortune (1216 AD)

8. English Civil War: Cannonballs, Courage, and Concealed Tunnels (1642-1646)

4.

9. Thriving Market Town: Barges, Breweries, and Bricks (Post-Civil War to Georgian Era)

10. Return Home - Modern Newark

At Rear: Newark On Trent – A Complete Journey Through Time (14,000 – Present)

& A Special Creative Treat :)

1. Introduction - Colette's Discovery

Colette was not your average, everyday, run-of-the-mill girl. Oh no. She had a mischievous sparkle in her eyes, a backpack that usually contained emergency biscuits and a slightly squashed banana, and a peculiar pocket watch.

This wasn't just any timepiece; it was made of gleaming brass and intricate gears that hummed softly when she held it, and it had a notorious habit of *not* just telling time, but actively *bending* it.

One gloriously sunny afternoon, the kind where dust motes danced in golden shafts of light, Colette found herself in her grandmother's attic.

It was a place of forgotten treasures and whispered secrets, smelling distinctly of old socks, forgotten biscuits (ironically, not her own), and the undeniable scent of adventure waiting to happen.

Amidst towering stacks of hatboxes and forgotten furniture draped in white sheets, her fingers brushed against something stiff and leather-bound. She tugged, and with a soft *thump*, a thick, surprisingly heavy book tumbled into her lap.

Its title, embossed in faded gold, read: **"The Wonderfully Wacky History of Newark-on-Trent."**

Colette's eyebrows shot up. "Fourteen thousand years?" she gasped, her eyes widening as she flipped to a page adorned with a rather grumpy-looking woolly mammoth. "That's older than Grandad's favourite (and very long) jokes!"

A mischievous grin spread across her face. Her hand instinctively reached for her pocket watch, its brass casing warming slightly in her palm. "Right then," she muttered to herself, her voice full of determination. "Operation: Newark Through the Ages is a GO!"

WHIZZ! POP! ZING!

The air crackled around her, the familiar attic walls blurring into streaks of colour, and a tingling sensation enveloped her from head to toe.

2. The Ice Age: Mammoth Mishaps and Flinty Fun (14,000 years ago)

Colette landed with an undignified *splat* in a surprisingly soft, yet incredibly cold, snowdrift. Her teeth began to chatter almost immediately.

"Brrr! Why, oh *why*, did I not pack my emergency mittens and a flask of hot chocolate?" she mumbled, rubbing her arms.

The landscape was stark and breathtaking: vast, rolling plains covered in snow and sparse, hardy trees. And then she saw them. Towering woolly mammoths, their shaggy coats dusted with snow, stomped past with the rhythmic thud of hairy buses. Their enormous tusks curled towards the icy sky, and their breath plumed in the freezing air. This was the true prehistoric hotspot of Farndon Fields, the prime hunting ground for these magnificent beasts and swift red deer.

A figure emerged from behind a snow-covered boulder, cloaked entirely in rough animal furs. He raised a hand in a surprisingly friendly wave. "Welcome, little traveler! I'm Thorgar. Or maybe Thurgle. Names are a bit tricky in this era, what with all the grunting and pointing." He had a booming laugh that seemed to shake the icicles from the trees.

Thorgar, or Thurgle, with remarkable patience, showed Colette how to expertly chip away at a piece of flint, demonstrating how to transform a simple stone into a sharp, essential tool for survival.

He explained how the mighty River Trent, though partially frozen, was their absolute lifeline – a source of fish, fresh water, and even, as he cheerfully put it, "a rather chilly place to wash our mammoth socks!"

Colette, determined to be helpful, picked up a sturdy piece of flint. She concentrated, chipping and tapping, trying to replicate Thorgar's swift, precise movements. After a few frustrating minutes, she proudly presented her creation.

It was undeniably blunt, perfectly round, and looked suspiciously like a very primitive, very lumpy spoon. Thorgar chuckled, patting her on the head. "Almost, little one. Almost."

WHIZZ! POP! ZING!

The cold air swirled, and the mammoths faded from view.

3. The Timber Circle: Ancient Raves and Sacred Spaces (4,000 years ago)

Colette's next landing was thankfully much softer, and the air was now warm and filled with the scent of damp earth and freshly cut wood.

The sky was a brilliant, cloudless blue, and the sound of grunting and rhythmic thuds filled the air.

Before her, a bustling community of people, clad in simple woven tunics, were engaged in an incredible feat of engineering: they were lifting enormous, rough-hewn wooden posts, thicker than tree trunks, into deep holes in the ground.

This was Middlebeck, and a truly monumental structure was taking shape.

A woman with wild, braided hair adorned with feathers and a curious necklace made of polished animal teeth approached Colette, a wide, earthy smile on her face. "We call it a henge," she announced, her voice resonating with pride. "It's a sacred place, built for the sun, the moon, and the spirits of our ancestors. It marks the seasons, guides our planting, and ensures good harvests." She paused, then added with a wink, "Also, it makes a truly fantastic place for a community feast and a bit of a party under the stars!"

Colette imagined ancient discos, where tribal beats echoed across the plains and people danced with joyous abandon around the towering timber circle.
As Colette watched, she noticed the immense effort involved. Each post was hoisted with ropes woven from plant fibres, pulled by many strong hands, a testament to collective strength and purpose. She also spotted smooth, polished axes, some made from stone from as far away as Cumbria, glinting in the sunlight – tools that helped shape these very posts.

Aella explained that this henge was also used for important ceremonies, including cremation burials, a respectful way to honour their dead. She saw a sense of deep connection to the land and the cosmos in their every movement.

Colette, feeling the infectious energy, skipped around the growing circle, imagining the grand ceremonies and vibrant gatherings that would take place here. It was a place where history was literally being built, post by post.

WHIZZ! POP! ZING!

The timber posts blurred, and the sounds of construction faded.

4. Roman Margidunum: Toasty Toes and Twelve Goats (43-410 AD)

Colette landed with a rather jarring jolt onto a perfectly straight, hard-packed road. It was surprisingly smooth, quite unlike the muddy tracks she'd seen in earlier times.

Before she could properly dust herself off, a loud, authoritative voice boomed, "By Jupiter! Look sharp there, citizen! Welcome to Margidunum!"

A man in shiny, segmented armour, a gladius (short sword) at his hip, and a rather impressive plume on his helmet, strode towards her. This was Marcus, a Roman soldier, and he looked every bit the disciplined, efficient warrior.

He explained that Newark, though never given a grand Roman name (which Marcus seemed to find quite "rude"), was a crucial stopping point along the Fosse Way, one of the primary Roman roads stretching across Britain.

This road connected settlements and forts, ensuring the swift movement of legions and trade.

Marcus, clearly proud of Roman ingenuity, gave Colette a whirlwind tour of a nearby Roman villa. She marvelled at the intricate mosaic floors, depicting scenes of mythology and daily life, pieced together from thousands of tiny coloured tiles. But what truly amazed her was the underfloor heating system, the hypocaust.

"We Romans," Marcus declared, puffing out his chest, "like our toes delightfully toasty, even when winter winds whistle through the province!"

He then pointed out the remains of large kilns in the distance. "And while we're talking about comfort, this area is famous for its pottery! We had over seventy-three pottery kilns here – it wasn't just a hobby, little one; it was a full-blown ceramic empire!"

He also mentioned the existence of fine Roman beer, and even, rather mysteriously, a dodecahedron found nearby. "Why? No one truly knows! Because why not?"

Colette, always up for a challenge, decided to try out her Latin, a few phrases she'd heard Marcus utter. She confidently announced

"Duodecim capras quaeso!"

Marcus stared, then burst into laughter. "Twelve goats, you say? Are you planning a Roman farm, little one?" Colette blushed, realizing her attempt at "How are you?" had gone hilariously awry.

WHIZZ! POP! ZING!

The straight road shimmered, and Marcus's laughter faded into the past.

5. Early St. Mary Magdalene Church: Mud, Mortar, and Monks (c. 11th Century)

Now she was in a muddy village full of hammering and shouting.

Colette's next destination deposited her in a bustling, muddy village. The air was thick with the sounds of hammering, the shouts of workmen, and the earthy smell of damp soil and fresh-cut timber. This was Newark in its early medieval form, a place where the town was slowly beginning to take shape around its burgeoning market.

A stout monk, his brown habit smudged with mortar and his beard liberally dusted with stone chips, offered her a weary but friendly smile. "Ah, welcome, young pilgrim! We are building a church, a grand place of worship for the people of Newark!" he declared, gesturing to the rising stone walls. "It will be a haven of peace, a place for solemn prayer, and, I'm sure, a rather popular residence for the local pigeons."

He explained that Newark was growing, becoming a "burh," a fortified town, and a church was central to its community and identity.

The town was even minting its own coins, a sign of its increasing importance as a trading hub. Colette noticed how the village was slowly transforming, with new buildings arising, and realised that many of the modern street names, like "Barnby Gate," actually had Norse origins, hinting at earlier Viking influences.

Colette, always eager to lend a hand, bravely attempted to help carry a rough-hewn stone block towards the rising walls.

She strained, her muscles aching, but the stone barely budged. It was heavier, she discovered, than her entire schoolbag after a particularly ambitious library visit – filled with textbooks, notebooks, and possibly a few extra (forgotten) snacks. The monk chuckled kindly. "Perhaps," he suggested, "you could fetch us some water instead, little one?"

WHIZZ! POP! ZING! The sounds of construction dissolved as the watch pulled her forward.

6. Newark Castle's Construction: Bishops, Battlements, and Builders (12th Century)

Colette gasped, her jaw dropping open at the awe-inspiring sight before her. Gone was the muddy village of simple wooden structures; now, a colossal stone castle, bristling with scaffolding and a hive of activity, dominated the landscape.

The air thrummed with the clang of hammers on stone, the shouts of overseers, and the rhythmic creak of wooden cranes.

Knights in gleaming, though somewhat dusty, chainmail clanked past, their spurs jingling, while ladies in elegant, colourful gowns strolled through the nascent courtyards, their laughter echoing amidst the construction noise.

The rich, savoury scent of roasting meat wafted from makeshift kitchens, adding to the vibrant atmosphere.

She spotted a figure of immense authority, resplendent in fine robes, overseeing the bustling scene with a keen eye.

This was Bishop Alexander the Magnificent, a powerful and ambitious man of the 12th century, known for his grand building projects.

A stern-faced guard, leaning on a newly finished battlement, explained to Colette that the castle wasn't just a grand residence; it was a strategic masterpiece. "His Lordship, Bishop Alexander," the guard intoned, "built this fortress to control the vital River Trent.

Any merchant barges passing through must now pay their tolls!" He added, with a wry grin, "And let me tell you, those taxes weren't always popular, but they were certainly profitable for the Bishop!"

Colette watched, fascinated, as masons meticulously shaped enormous stone blocks, lifting them into place with surprising precision.

The castle was clearly designed to be formidable, a statement of power and a guardian of the waterway.

She could almost feel the weight of history being laid stone by stone, each block a piece of Newark's growing might.

WHIZZ! POP! ZING!

The sounds of construction faded, replaced by an ominous hush.

7. King John at Newark Castle: Whispers of Loss and Royal Ill-Fortune (1216 AD)

Colette landed with a soft thump near a bustling, ancient bridge spanning the River Trent. The air, however, was thick with a palpable tension, a hushed anxiety that seemed to cling to the cobbled streets.

People moved with hurried steps, their faces etched with worry, whispering in hushed tones about "the King" and "the Great Charter." This was 1216, and the turbulent reign of King John was drawing to a close.

Suddenly, a somber procession approached. Colette saw him: King John himself, looking pale, drawn, and intensely irritable, slumped in a litter carried by weary servants.

He was clearly very ill, his face flushed with fever, and his eyes had a vacant, troubled look. He was being brought to Newark Castle, a place where he would soon meet his infamous end.

The whispers around Colette grew louder: "Dysentery, they say..." and "His last journey..."

A merchant, his face creased with concern, leaned closer to Colette, his voice low. "Terrible luck, that King John," he muttered. "Lost his entire baggage train, including the Crown Jewels and all his treasure, in the treacherous tidal waters of The Wash!

A truly unfortunate event, that. Some say it was a curse for signing that Magna Carta, others say just bad tides and worse judgment." The merchant shook his head, a mixture of pity and exasperation in his eyes.

The sheer misfortune seemed to cling to the King, a heavy cloak of ill-omens. Colette felt a shiver despite the relatively mild weather – the weight of history and impending doom hung heavy in the air.

WHIZZ! POP! ZING!

The murmurs of the past faded as the watch propelled her onward.

8. English Civil War: Cannonballs, Courage, and Concealed Tunnels (1642-1646)

Colette spun the pocket watch again, feeling the familiar tingle. This time, her landing was anything but gentle; she practically ducked as a terrifying *CRUMP* sounded nearby, followed by the whistle of something heavy flying overhead. Newark was no longer a peaceful market town.

It was a chaotic, dangerous mess of cannons, hastily dug trenches, and soldiers in strange, yet vibrant, colourful uniforms – Royalist red contrasting with Parliamentarian blue. "For King Charles!" a gritty voice roared, and a small company of soldiers, muskets at the ready, dashed past her.

It was the English Civil War, and Newark was right at the heart of the conflict. It was a fiercely loyal Royalist stronghold, meaning the town staunchly supported King Charles I against the Parliamentarian forces.

Because of its strategic location and unwavering loyalty, Newark became one of the most besieged towns in England, enduring *three* relentless sieges.

Colette saw firsthand the desperate conditions: cannonballs whistling through the air, damaging buildings, the constant threat of attack, and the grim reality of starvation within the besieged walls. Locals were enduring not just physical hardship but also, as the historical records wryly noted, "probably some very bad hair days" due to the endless conflict.

She learned about the incredible resilience of the townsfolk and soldiers. They dug secret tunnels beneath the town, not just for escape but also for launching surprise attacks on the besieging Parliamentarians.

The castle, despite being battered and scarred by cannon fire, held strong for years, a defiant symbol of Royalist resistance. But eventually, with resources dwindling and the King's cause fading, King Charles I himself sent word for Newark to surrender.

It was a heart-wrenching moment for the brave defenders, but they had held out longer than almost any other Royalist garrison. Colette felt the grit and determination of these historical figures, living through such a tumultuous time.

WHIZZ! POP! ZING!

The echoes of cannon fire softened, giving way to the bustle of recovery.

9. Thriving Market Town: Barges, Breweries, and Bricks (Post-Civil War to Georgian Era)

Colette's next stop brought a welcome sense of peace, though the landscape still bore scars. The magnificent castle, once a defiant symbol of strength, was now a majestic ruin, its walls breached, a testament to the war's destructive power. Yet, despite the damage, the town was vibrantly alive, buzzing with renewed energy. This was Newark recovering, entering an era of prosperity and growth, especially during the Georgian period.

The River Trent, no longer a battleground, was a bustling highway of commerce. Barges, heavily laden with goods, sailed serenely downstream. Colette saw huge bales of wool, sacks of corn, and various other vital commodities destined for distant markets.

Newark was once known for its textiles, with Flemish weavers making it "the Milan of medieval England" for its fine wool production, and now trade was flourishing again.
She strolled through a lively market square, now dominated by handsome brick buildings, a stark contrast to earlier timber structures.

The air was filled with the shouts of vendors, the haggling of buyers, and the tantalizing aromas of fresh produce and baking bread. This was the town's social hub, a place of not just trade, but also lively gossip and community gatherings.

Colette paused outside the iconic Saracen's Head Inn, its grand sign creaking gently in the breeze. The inn was a hive of activity, its windows glowing warmly, revealing a bustling interior. Travelers from distant lands mingled with local merchants and townsfolk, sharing news, making deals, and undoubtedly enjoying a pint or two. Indeed, beer was still a major food group in Newark, keeping spirits high!

This was a time of enlightenment and refinement, where elegant coffee houses began to appear, inviting intellectual discussions and polite chit-chat. Newark, having survived its trials, had truly put on a "Georgian Glow-Up," becoming stylish, intellectual, and, perhaps, just a little bit smug about its newfound prosperity.

Finally, Colette sighed, the vibrant past swirling around her. It was time. With a determined flick of her wrist, she set her pocket watch for home.

WHIZZ! POP! ZING!

The past dissolved into a familiar haze.

10. Return Home - Modern Newark

Back in her own time, the familiar scent of old socks and forgotten biscuits (her grandmother's attic) filled her nostrils. Colette took a deep breath, the adventure still tingling in her fingers. She immediately pulled out her phone and searched for "Newark-on-Trent." Her first stop? The castle ruins.

Walking through the ancient archways, she found the castle to be a place of serene beauty, its weathered stones basking peacefully in the modern sunlight. No longer a fortress under siege, it was a tranquil park, a place for quiet reflection and family picnics.

She looked at the mighty River Trent, now calm and unburdened by battle or heavy barges, and imagined the woolly mammoths, the Roman soldiers, the medieval builders, the anxious townsfolk during the sieges, and the bustling Georgian merchants who had all lived, loved, and shaped this very spot.

She thought of the Civil War Centre, a modern testament to Newark's dramatic past, and chuckled, remembering how the town's "quirks" had even gone viral on social media. From ancient flint tools to modern broadband, from Bronze Age bling to Facebook fame, Newark had truly seen it all.

"Newark," she whispered, her voice filled with awe and affection, "you are truly a story that never ends!"

With a happy sigh, Colette carefully tucked her wonderfully wacky pocket watch back into its special velvet pouch. She knew this wasn't the end of her adventures, merely a pause.

The history of Newark, she understood now, wasn't just in old books or crumbling ruins; it was a living, breathing narrative, continually unfolding, waiting for new chapters to be written, and new explorers like her to discover them.

She was ready for her next magical journey, knowing that the spirit of adventure, and the enduring story of places like Newark, would always continue.

The End

Newark On Trent – A Complete Journey Through Time

14,000 BC – The Original Flintstones
Cavemen rocked up with flint tools and a dream. Farndon Fields was the prehistoric hotspot for hunting mammoths and red deer. Basically, Newark was the Stone Age's version of Center Parcs.

10,000–3300 BC – From Spears to Spades
Mesolithic folks brought tiny arrow bits (microliths), then Neolithic types said, "Let's settle down," invented farming, and started the first allotments. One axe even got recycled into a whetstone. Ecowarriors before it was cool.

3300–700 BC – Bronze Age Bling
Middlebeck revealed a henge (prehistoric VIP lounge), 35 cremation burials, and a polished axe from Cumbria. Clearly, Newark was the place to be buried and accessorised.

800 BC–43 AD – Iron Age Swag
The Corieltauvi tribe farmed, forged, and flaunted gold torcs. Newark's Iron Age residents had roundhouses, loom weights, and serious jewellery game. The Newark Torc? Total Iron Age haute couture.

43–410 AD – Romans: Pottery, Please
Newark didn't get a Roman name (rude), but it did get 73 pottery kilns. That's not a hobby, that's a fullblown ceramic empire. Also: beer, villas, and a dodecahedron. Because why not?

410–1066 AD – Saxons, Vikings & Lady Godiva
Newark became a "burh" (fortified town), minted coins, and hosted over 300 urns. Street names like "Barnby Gate" come from Norse. Oh, and Lady Godiva owned the place. Yes, that Lady Godiva.

1066–1485 – Medieval Mayhem
Newark Castle was built, King John died here (with dysentery, no less), and the town got its market moved to Wednesday. Also: knights, fairs, and a battle called "Lincoln Fair" (yes, really).

1485–1603 – Tudor Textiles & Tavern Tales
Wool was king. Flemish weavers made Newark the Milan of medieval England. Inns popped up, floods knocked down bridges, and the Battle of Stoke Field ended the Wars of the Roses just outside town.

1603–1714 – Stuart Shenanigans
Newark got sieged three times during the Civil War. The castle held strong, but eventually surrendered when King Charles I said "enough." Locals endured cannonballs, starvation, and probably some very bad hair days.

1714–1837 – Georgian Glow-Up

Brick buildings, posh coffee houses, and Enlightenment chit-chat. Newark got stylish, intellectual, andslightly smug. The Town Hall and Market thrived, and beer was still a major food group.

1837–1901 – Victorian Vibes

Trains arrived, factories boomed, and Newark ironworks made everything from bearings to banisters. Sanitation improved (finally), and the town got a proper glow-up with Gothic spires and civic pride.

1900s – Wars, Floods & Rock 'n' Roll

Two world wars, a factory bombing, and a royal visit. Newark powered through with grit, jazz, and a lot of tea. The 1960s brought dance halls, denim, and dreams of the future.

2000s – Digital Newark & Facebook Fame

Newark entered the 21st century with broadband, baristas, and a booming photo group. The Civil War Centre opened, glamping took off, and the town's quirks went viral. History, meet hashtags.

A Special Creative Treat

Have fun!
:)

All pictures converted from Photos taken by Dave Fargher

To purchase the full version of the colouring book visit
www.newarkguide.co.uk/shop

Discover Newark-on-Trent like never before with this fun and educational colouring book!

Perfect for kids and curious minds of all ages, this beautifully designed book features **10 detailed illustrations of Newark's most iconic historic sites with descriptions** — ready for you to bring to life with colour,.

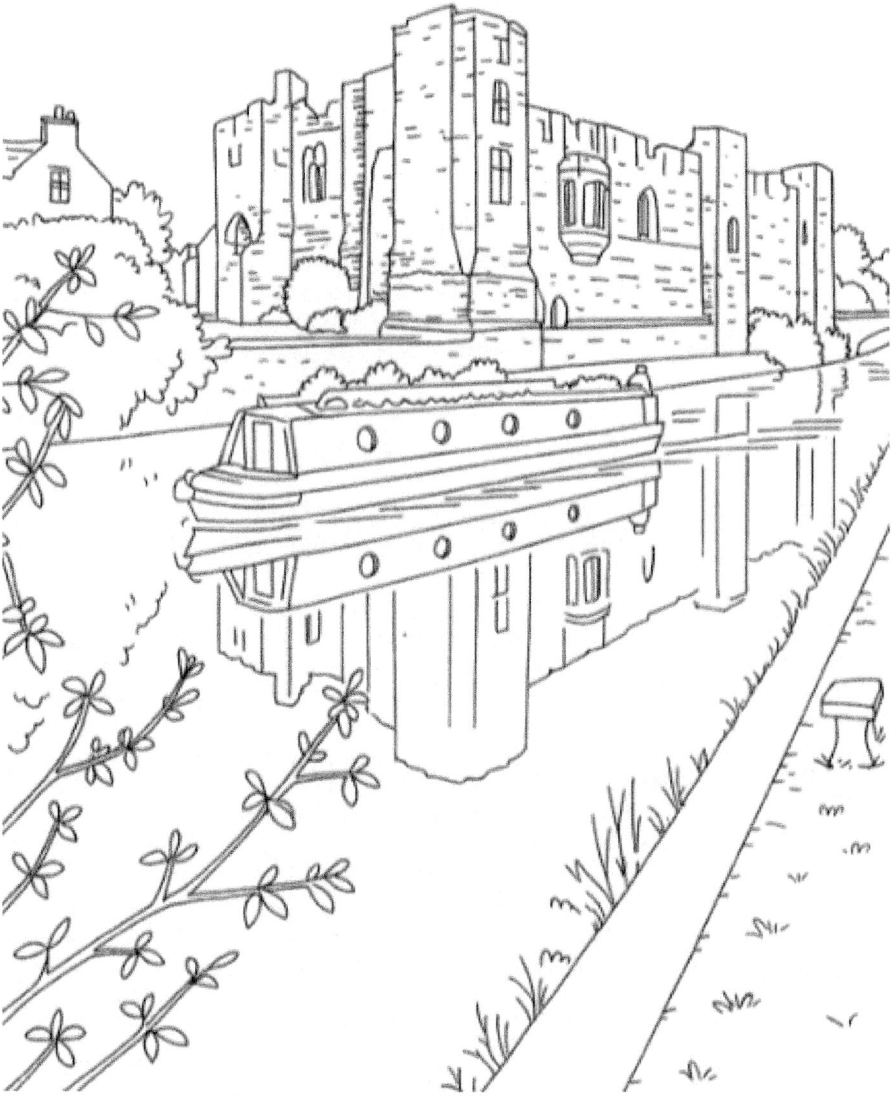

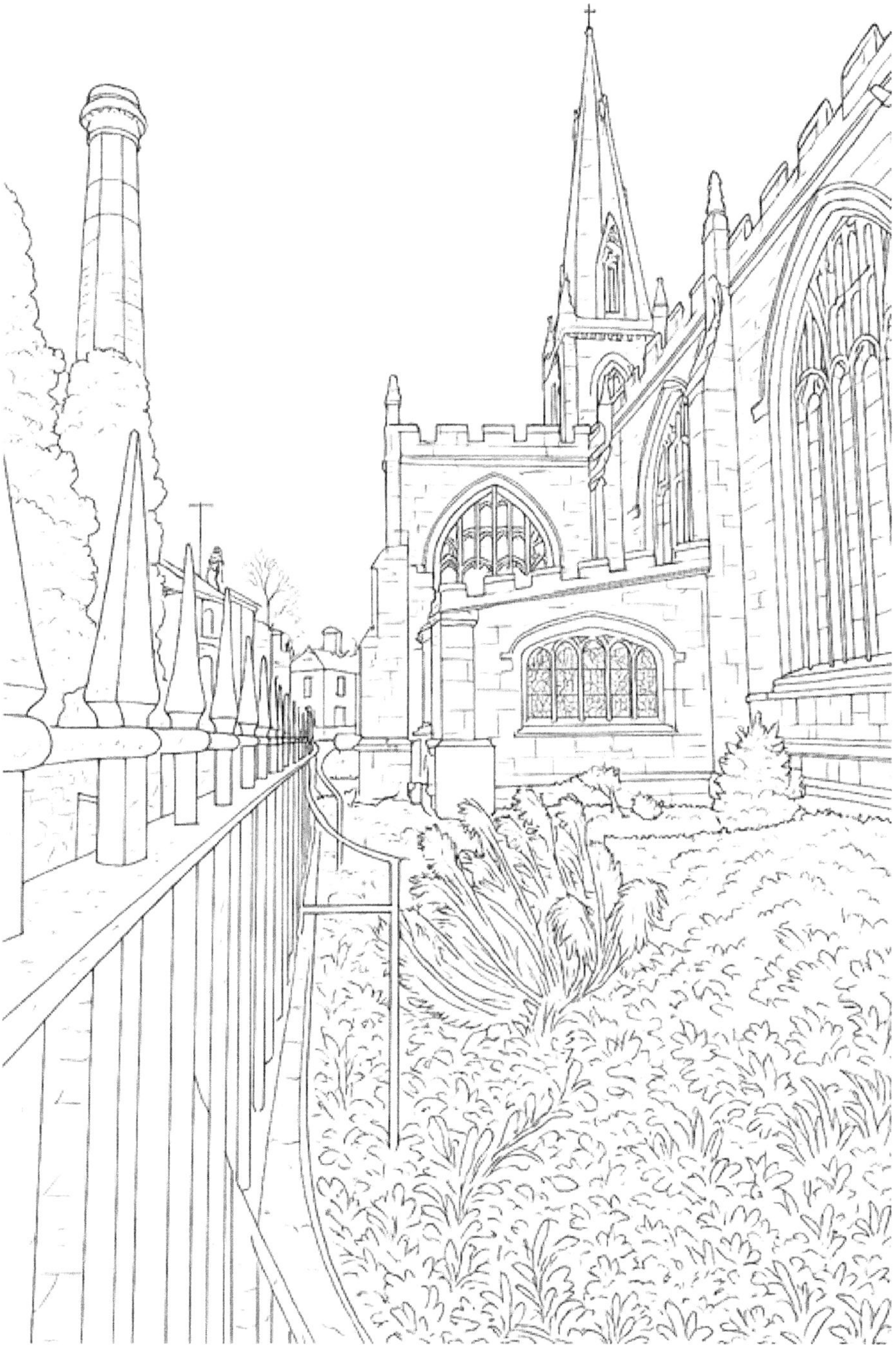

To Purchase my full book

"Newark On Trent: A Sometimes Witty Journey Through Time".

Visit the shop - www.newarkguide.co.uk/shop

14,000 Years of History, One Town, and More Puns Than You Can Shake a Saxon at.

Available in Paperback, Hardback and ebook

Ever wondered what happens when you mix mammoth hunters, Roman potters, Viking landlords, Questionable kings, Civil War cannonballs, and a 21st-century 40 something bloke with a sarcasm problem and a potential mid life crisis?

You get this book!

Written by local and self-declared "heritage whisperer" Dave Fargher, this is Newark-on-Trent's entire history — told with wit, warmth, and a healthy disrespect for dusty textbooks.

From flint tools to fibre broadband, this book takes you on a whirlwind tour through the town's prehistoric party pads, medieval mayhem, Tudor textiles, Victorian viaducts, and digital-age delights.

Who's it for?
History lovers who like their facts with a side of fun. .Locals who've walked past Newark Castle a thousand times and still don't know why King John died there (spoiler: it wasn't the food). Visitors who want to know what makes this market town tick (and occasionally explode). Anyone who thinks history should be more pub chat than PowerPoint.

Why buy it?
Because Newark's story deserves to be told — and laughed at. It's a 100 page tale of resilience, reinvention, and really questionable royal decisions. Plus, it's packed with fascinating facts, forgotten legends, and enough puns to make a Saxon blush.

So grab a copy, grab a cuppa (or a pint), and prepare to fall in love with Newark-on-Trent — one witty, wonderful chapter at a time.

The Book also contains a wealth of additional resource too:

A complete timeline of Newarks History
Former Factories
Historic sites and points of interest
The Myth of The Newark Tunnels
The Story of Newarks walls and gates

Designed and Created by Dave Fargher

Printed in Dunstable, United Kingdom